Storytelling Through Video

7 Steps for Producing & Promoting Video Content

Patrick Fuller

ISBN: 9781088510636

DEDICATION

This book is dedicated to every single entrepreneur, business owner, and marketing minded person who is passionate about their business and getting their name of there. You are the people that ooze passion and excitement and truly try to make the world a better place.

Keep doing, keep creating, keep pushing forward… your big break will happen, and I hope this book offers a little help in getting there!

CONTENTS

ACKNOWLEDGMENTS

By far the most important person in my journey has been and will continue to be my amazing wife, Joy. To say, "Thank You" doesn't seem like it's powerful enough if I'm being completely honest. Not only did she help edit this book and ask a ton of great questions (which will turn into video content by the way!) but she's been completely supportive in everything I do… and trust me when I tell you that's not easy. In fact, I'm not easy to live with. I'm driven almost to a fault and she's there to support me. I'm a (calculated) risk taker and she's there to support me. I'm a dreamer and she's there to support me. I work through problems and issues by working out (CrossFit) and she's there to support me. Life hasn't been as easy as I may want you to believe and yet she is right there supporting me. We would all be so lucky as to have a Joy in our lives.

To my kids, Preston and Cassidy. I love you so much it hurts! Thank you for letting me film your soccer games and work out sessions at the gym. Thank you for asking so many questions and being so curious about life. Thank you for understanding that there are just times that Dad has to work, and he can't play with you. But mostly, thank you for being such great kids!

To my parents, I know you don't always understand what I do, or how we are getting by, but I really appreciate all of the love and support. Whether it's helping me make sound panels for the studio or watching the kids so I can write or film you're always there to support us. The kids love you, Joy loves you, and I love you very much.

Without my friend Pam Metivier, this book would honestly never have happened. Pam is a marketing strategy and social ads genius. She is also the co-author of STEAMTeam 5, a book for young girls about Science, Technology, Engineering, Art and Math. Not only has Pam done most of the editing for the book, she has been a sounding board, an entrepreneur interview participant, a promoter, a conduit for new business, and a friend. Pam, I cannot thank you enough for your support over the years and I hope we continue to experiment and do big things together for a very long time.

This book isn't about CrossFit or working out, but without those things I wouldn't be who I am today, let alone be able to use concepts and ideas found within them to change my life and my health. At the center of all that learning, experimentation, and growing is Melissa Patriquin. Melissa has been my CrossFit coach for a couple of years and epitomizes "sticking to the plan", "small progressions every day", and "keep experimenting."

Last but not least, I'd like to say 'Thank You' to two people I may never actually see again, as odd as that sounds. A few years ago, when I was trying to figure out how to market a SAAS product my company built, I was running out of money, didn't know who I could trust to help me tell my story with video, and didn't actually own a camera. I had never used YouTube before and I came across Meredith Marsh and Peter McKinnon. Meredith had just released a series of 30 videos she called, "30 days of GoPro - A Guide for Beginners" and through watching those videos I felt like I could operate a camera and create content… it was the beginning of a new chapter in my life.

When I discovered Peter McKinnon, he had less than 500K subscribers (he has nearly 4M now) and his ability to talk to a camera and teach and entertain are like nothing I have ever experienced. He changed the way I thought about content, quality, and having fun doing it. I had a chance to meet them both at a conference in 2018 and they were just as genuine and authentic as in their videos. Everyone has to start somewhere and having people to guide you along the way is an amazing experience, something I hope to continue with this book.

INTRODUCTION

Video is often cited as the most effective marketing content for driving results. It's proven to significantly increase website traffic, time on site, social engagement, and conversion. But it's not only a great marketing tool. Videos also play a significant role in closing sales as well as customer training and support. So, we're all in agreement that video is important. Now what?

I constantly hear business leaders say, "We've always wanted to do video, but we didn't know someone we could trust, we didn't know what we were doing, and we didn't know how much it should cost." The goal of this book is to help you answer all these questions—and more!

In my consulting practice, I guide clients through a 7-step process to help them answer the following **five key questions**:

What role should video play in meeting our business goals?

What types of videos do we need?

How do we tell the most compelling story?

Who or what should be the subject of our video(s)?

What should our video marketing strategy be?

In the following chapters, I'm going to walk you through a tried-and-true, 7-step process for planning, producing, and promoting video content online.

VIDEO UPLOADING...

1 | THE 7-STEP PROCESS

I use a proven 7-step process at Fuller Story to ensure our video strategy and production projects run smoothly. There's a lot of planning and preparation that needs to take place to produce great video content.

In this book, I'll walk through each of these steps and offer my tips and advice for completing each one.

Step 1: Story Discovery

For consultants like me, it's important we perform market research and conduct interviews with key stakeholders to learn about our client's business goals and marketing objectives as the very first step in developing a video strategy. This is where we hear our client's story in their own words. Even if you're using internal resources for all of your video needs, I recommended you start with the story you want to tell.

Step 2: Developing the Video Strategy

The second step involves developing a plan that includes all the types of video(s) and video/story concepts you'll need to meet your goals as well as suggestions for who to include in the videos and where to film your video session(s). It's a good idea to plan ahead by determining what types of B-roll content you'll need to have. (I'll explain the importance of B-roll later.)

Quick tip: Don't use an agency who uses a "cookie cutter" video plan for all of their clients. You want a plan designed with your company's specific business and marketing goals in mind. At Fuller Story, we make recommendations for video themes, content, formats, etc., based on each clients' organization.

Step 3: Filming Prep

During this step, you should draft the initial talking points (or scripts), flow, and imagery for each video you're producing. We allow clients to edit to their heart's content during this step, and we provide feedback along the way.

Step 4: Filming Session

The filming session can be the most fun part of the process—if you plan well. I recommend scheduling and preparing all participants for your filming session(s) beforehand so they're as comfortable as possible. People tell us that our filming sessions are a lot more fun than they expected! I'll share my tips for a successful (and fun) session.

Step 5: Editing & Revisions

This is where the real magic happens. It's also the step where you'll spend the most time. In this book, I'll cover my tips and tricks for editing that will save you a ton of time.

Step 6: Video Production

During this phase, you'll put the final touches on your video(s) and prepare them for publishing.

Step 7: Video Marketing

Once your videos are in the right format for sharing, you'll be ready to use them in marketing campaigns. I'll provide an overview of how video marketing works in this book.

2 | THE ART OF GOOD STORYTELLING

Everyone loves a good story. So, how do you tell a story about your business, your cause, your product, or you that captures and holds someone's attention? As marketers, we can show—and tell—a compelling story in mere seconds using videos. In this chapter, I'm going to explain the different types of stories you can tell using different types of videos.

TYPES OF VIDEOS

There is nearly an unlimited amount of video content you could produce to create value for your customers. I always recommend that all businesses create at least these three: product explainer, customer testimonial, and company story.

These three videos help define who you are, give prospective customers an idea of what they should expect, and humanize the CEO/founder(s) or leadership team. It is really no different than if you were to meet someone new in person. You would naturally give them a sense of who you are just by the way you communicate and how passionate you are when you talk about what you do.

When prospective customers come to your website or social media presence without videos, they won't have the same feeling and experience as when they meet you in person. These first three videos bridge that gap. And, let's be honest, the videos scale a heck of a lot better than trying to meet everyone.

Here is a bit more information on each of these main types of videos.

Product Explainer Video

Think about the last time you browsed around a company's website and thought to yourself: "Is this business even legit? What the heck do they do?"

This is the last impression you want to leave on a site visitor or potential customer, which is why a product explainer video is the first video you should make. This video doesn't simply showcase all the best features you have to offer. Instead, it should paint a picture that clearly points to a problem your solution can solve.

Appeal to viewers' emotions and explain how your solution can help make their lives easier, better, more fulfilling—whatever the case may be—and you're on your way to seeing success with video.

Product explainer videos answer the questions, "What the heck do you do?" or "What the heck does this product do, and why do I care?" The goal isn't to just talk about all the "cool" features your product or service has. It should convey the problem it is solving, and it should appeal to the viewers' emotions by explaining how the solution can help make their lives easier, better, and more fulfilling.

Customer Testimonial Video

What's great about testimonial videos is that you only need one or two solid ones in your catalogue to see the difference they can make.

Seek out some of your long-term customers that have seen tangible results thanks to your product or service. Consider customers who would tell a compelling story, not just "we use it, it's great." You're looking for tangible results, an "ah ha" moment, and the ability to articulate how using your product or service has changed things for them.

Ideally, your prospects will be able to see themselves and their businesses in the testimonial videos you create. Ultimately, video testimonials help visitors feel more confident in your business and the services you provide. And why wouldn't they? Your most authentic subjects are your actual customers.

Customer testimonial videos help build trust and confidence with prospective customers. The idea is to humanize the existing customer and make the viewer feel like "that could be me" in the sense that they solved a problem they currently have or are in the position or industry the customer is also in. This also gives the viewer an idea of how Customer A uses the product/service and gives them a frame of reference around what they like about the product/service or what kind of an impact the product/service had for them.

Company Story Video

How did your business get started? What was your motivation for starting the company? By featuring the friendly faces of your leadership team and teammates, you can make your prospects feel right at home.

People are more likely to buy products and services based on emotion rather than logic, which is why telling your story is so important. They get "the why" and resonate with what you've set out to do. A company story video lets you show off what makes your business so special and unique on a human level.

Outside of creating unique video content that helps educate, entertain and inspire your prospective customers here is a list of videos to help drive awareness, trust and authority.

Company Overview Video

Company overview videos make the company the main focal point. Think of it as your company's origin—a backstory that conveys your unique history. This type of video will usually have one speaker (who does not have to be the entrepreneur or the CEO) who can tell the company story extremely well. B-Roll is typically used to highlight the company headquarters, the people, or the product.

In addition to the main three types of videos described above, I recommend using the following videos if they're relevant to your specific goals and objectives.

Recruitment Video

Recruitment videos can be used to entice prospective employees to want to work for the company. This video will feel like a promo video for the company and how great it is to work there. It can be broken into two parts, where the first part can be used over and over (such as an intro) and the second part to be swapped out with specifics around what the company is hiring for, timing, etc. (This makes the video more time relevant and specific.)

Entrepreneur Story Video

Entrepreneur story videos help entrepreneurs/founders share their background and experience. The idea is to humanize the entrepreneur and enable them to share their story in a more personal way.

Short video clips can be used in advertising and email campaigns as well as on landing pages as teasers. These videos can add a real element of personalization to landing pages and funnel sequences as well.

Fundraiser Video

Fundraiser videos are the next generation of a Pitch Deck or an Investor Deck. The video incorporates a bit of the entrepreneur's story with the charts/graphs/metrics of the traditional pitch deck. These types of videos can be very effective when you include B-Roll of the product and or short customer testimonials.

Event Video

Posting videos of your events is a great way to bring the fun of the occasion to those who couldn't make it. It's also a good way to showcase where you play and what you're all about.

Event videos like these are fantastic to drive associations with other industry leaders as well as influencers. They can also be used as a "behind the scenes" look at a particular operation or segment of your business and allow the viewer to feel like they are getting a special VIP experience. Ultimately, these types of videos help viewers and prospective customers build a tighter bond with you.

Educational Content Video

I consider educational videos a "must have" for all companies because they help you establish your organization as a thought leader. This type of video content is quickly replacing text-based blogs. The key to these types of videos is consistency. Creating weekly or monthly vlogs on various topics could get you a loyal audience and following, eager to tune in for the next installment.

All of the videos I've described serve a unique purpose. But when it comes to creating long-term value, educational videos are often the best investment. This type of video content is meant to be continuous, albeit in smaller chunks.

When I help companies create a strategy for educational video content, we try to keep the theme or content of the video into two or three categories. This allows us to brainstorm multiple topics within each category and weave them all into a central theme. The central theme could be education, or entertainment, or even all the different uses for their product or service.

You're probably thinking that this type of content seems familiar. The reason for this is because, if you're an online marketer, you've probably followed this same best practice during your content marketing planning.

The biggest difference now is that—you guessed it! —you get to add a face and a personality to the content for your customers. You get to be more entertaining and informative and add visuals to further explain, bolster, and conceptualize the point.

So now that you know what types of video you want to create, how do you go about filming them in the best possible way that creates great quality but also minimizes your time commitment and need for additional shooting retakes? (Hint, I'll cover that in the next chapter!)

See some examples of each of these videos and the strategy behind them on the Fuller Story Website: https://fullerstory.com/case-studies.

3 | DEVELOPING A VIDEO CONTENT STRATEGY

Simply put, developing a video content strategy involves determining what types of videos you need to produce based on your business and marketing goals. For example, you might need a video to demonstrate the core features of your product to encourage someone to purchase it. Or, you might want to use customer testimonial videos in LinkedIn advertising campaigns to attract prospective leads for your company.

In this chapter, I'm going to explain how to develop a video content strategy and begin planning for production.

Let's start with **WHY**. Why do you want to add video content to your existing marketing efforts? If I ask 12 people this question, I would likely get a dozen different answers. In the end, it should really come down to one thing: creating a better connection with both your prospective audience (prospects) and your existing audience (customers).

Video allows your customers to interact with your brand and business, ultimately helping them feel more comfortable with you.

By now, you're probably no stranger to seeing video in social media, social ads, and from the brands you love and respect. Sometimes we see these videos from the perspective of a consumer and sometimes from a pure entertainment perspective. But did you know that half of consumers who watch online product videos say it helps them make more confident purchasing decisions and develop a greater sense of trust with both the product/service and the company?

Adding videos to your landing pages can increase conversion rates by 80%! And the mere mention of the word "video" in your email subject line has shown to increase open rates by 19%.

Here are a few more video related metrics that will blow your mind:

- 65% of people are visual learners, yet our primary form of communication is often words (emails, newsletters, etc.).

- 74% of users who watched an explainer video about a product subsequently bought it.

- Video supercharges email click-through rates by up to 300% on average.

So now that we've established WHY we want to incorporate video into our existing marketing strategy, let's talk about WHAT steps we need to follow and HOW we go about completing them.

You didn't start your business before you had a plan, you didn't start hiring the best resources without first knowing what and who you needed, and you didn't start acquiring customers without some idea of who you were going after and why—and video production is no different. Repeat with me: "I will have a plan before I push the record button!"

Every good business plan starts with a strategy. And your video strategy should incorporate the following:

- Who will be the go-to-contact for all things video production? This can be a single person or a team, but someone must be accountable.

- What will our video mission statement be? Trust me on this one. Once you get going, it will be very easy to veer off course. You'll want—no, need—a north star to be able to go back to from time to time.

- Are there important dates we need to consider? Think about the conferences/trade shows you attend. Do you have a new product or service launch coming up? What other company milestones, events, or anniversaries are happening in the next 12 months? These are all dates to consider for both video production and resource availability.

- How much can you afford to spend on video? You would be surprised how many companies I talk to that make a verbal commitment to video content but never allocate budget for it. It's like planning a trip, starting your journey, and not filling up the gas tank. Yes, video costs money just like all other marketing efforts. But it doesn't have to break the bank (more on that later).

- How will video augment or support existing marketing efforts? I've only met a handful of successful, more-than-one-person companies that do ZERO marketing. Everyone else does some level of marketing. Maybe you're on the smaller end with a website, a monthly email newsletter, and an occasional social media post. Maybe you're on the larger end with landing pages, marketing funnels with automated email marketing, a full social media team, and a marketing to-do list a mile long. Either way, video should help all of your existing efforts, not run parallel to them.

- Where should our video content live? Businesses who commit to video content have an average of 293 videos in their library. That is a pretty good size library, in both quantity and gigabytes! Whether you host on Vimeo, YouTube, or perhaps your own web site, consider how you could possibly double dip both the hosting and SEO. Did you know that YouTube is the second largest search site? Just saying!

- How will we measure the performance of our videos? Although a form of art, video performance can in fact be measured regardless of what your "creative team" may say! (Wink, wink!) I'm a really big fan of capturing as much data as I can, measuring everything that makes sense and constantly finding data points to tweak. That said, there are a few video performance measurements I live by outside of the traditional leads, time of page, and bounce rate measurements. More on those later.

- At what point should we reassess our current strategy? Personally, I love this question because it usually comes up when we did a poor job with all of the previous questions! It will be very easy and tempting to say "It's not working" after a few videos go live and you don't see a flood of new customers pouring in. Just like your business strategy, you have to give it time. And if you planned well enough, measured well enough, allocated enough budget, and have a guiding light as to why you started producing video content in the

21

first place, this question will answer itself.

BUDGETS

Since money is typically the biggest question on most everyone's mind, let's dive a little deeper into this topic. Ultimately you have three options when it comes to spending money.

Option 1 is to create a video department with internal staff, equipment, space allocation, software, tools and training. Basically, you're creating a mini-video production company inside of your existing company.

The upside to this option is that you can control every aspect of the process, the budget and the timeline. The downside to this option is that the initial investment (and continuous on-going investment, for that matter) is quite large when you consider all of the equipment, staff, training, software, and extra space and/or travel expenses.

With Option 1, you must decide what "good enough" is when it comes to skilled labor and your ability to pay them on a full-time basis. I don't have any issues with this approach. In fact, I've been called in more times than I can count to help companies like this get set up correctly and running efficiently. One thing I see too often, though, are companies who have committed to setting up their own video production department, but have hired inexperienced staff, purchased low-budget equipment, and/or committed the equivalent of a broom closet for a set. As a result, they're disappointed in the quality, time to market, and "wow factor" they're able to produce.

The costs associated with Option 1 depend on a number of factors (such as the number and types of videos you want to produce and the costs of resources in your area), but I've included a sample estimate on the following page.

Sample Cost for Option 1 – In-House

- Internal staff
    - Videographer/Editor ~ $50K
    - Marketing Coordinator ~ $45K
- Equipment ~$16K
    - Studio setup ~ $4K
    - Camera gear ~ $4.5K
    - Mobile video gear ~ $2K
    - Audio gear ~ $2.5K
    - Set design ~ $3K
- Space allocation ~$1K/mo
    - $20/sq ft x 500 sq ft
- Software & tools ~ $1K/mo.
- Training ~ $3K/yr.
- Misc (10%) ~ $13.5K
- TOTAL ~ $148.5K/year

Option 2 is exactly the opposite of Option 1 in that you hire a video production company for your video content. The upside to this option is that you only pay for what you need, meaning you don't have full-time staff sitting around costing you money when things are slow or held up. The downside is that your cost to produce videos will naturally go up (the video production company needs to make money too!), and it can be hard to know whom to trust—not just to do a good job but to help guide your video strategy, constantly come up with creative ideas, and remove the stress of production.

With Option 2, be sure to choose someone that can help you develop both a short-term and long-term strategy. Find someone who follows trends and can offer up ideas and other ways to add value. Do you go with a big, full-service agency or with a local boutique who specializes in video production? Who will create all of the social media video and related image assets? These are all questions you'll need to answer, and if you don't get it right it could cost you not just money but valuable time.

Sample Cost for Option 2 – 100% Outsourced Video Strategy & Production

- Average number of videos per year ~ 30
- Average price per video ~$6K
- Estimated total price ~$180K/year

As a fan of Venn diagrams, I try to find a third option for the companies I work with. **Option 3** is a hybrid of Option 1 and Option 2, where we identify existing resources (usually staff and possibly location/set) and marry them with my video production team. What makes it work for us is the partnership approach—not just in the definition but in the communication, integration, and transparency.

For example, let's say you already have an existing marketing team with a small social media team/person. You already have a marketing strategy you're currently executing and a social media presence. What most clients want is a company they can trust to help them put together a video production plan, create a smooth and comfortable filming experience, and produce quality videos and social media assets to be handed over to their existing team for execution. That said, the hybrid approach is not one-size-fits-all. Every company is unique in terms of business stage, degree of customer awareness, organization size and marketing budget, so every approach must also be different... and flexible!

Sample Cost for Option 3 – Work w/ a Partner to Develop Video Strategy w/ Outsourced Production (Hybrid Model)

- Fuller Story flat-rate monthly subscription ~$4K - $5K (w/ annual agreement)
  - o One filming session per month, 2-3 hours
  - o As many videos as possible produced within the filming session
  - o Additional filming sessions available at a discount
  - o Total = $48K-$60K/year

VIDEO HOSTING

The second most common question I get from companies I work with is, "Where should we host our video content?"

There are reasons to host video content in three primary platforms, and I like to get as much benefit out of where we host our content as possible.

More times than not, I choose to host video content on YouTube for one primary reason: searchability. Everyone knows that Google is the world's largest search engine, but most people don't know that YouTube is the second largest search engine (and is owned by Google). YouTube is becoming so popular as a search engine that Google is now showing YouTube search results as part of its "above the fold" results.

YouTube enables you to produce content that attracts and retains attention, so it should definitely be part of your search engine optimization plan. And while I could go on and on about YouTube, its algorithm, the built-in metrics it offers, the value of thumbnails, and how you leverage the platform to turn your video production from a cost center to a profit center, it also has a few drawbacks.

The biggest drawback for me when it comes to YouTube is after the video is done playing and your viewer is met with the "recommended videos" screen. You have no control over what is shown here and for me, that is one reason to consider using Vimeo. Vimeo gives you a bit more control over things like player customization, privacy controls, review/approval workflow, player calls-to-action and live event streaming, but you pay for these features.

Vimeo has a few different tiers of their service. Currently, they have five different tiers ranging from free (Vimeo Basic) to $75/mo. (Vimeo Premium). The biggest thing that separates these tiers, and Vimeo from YouTube, is the storage and upload limits. The Business tier also has the ability to integrate with Google Analytics and provide some level of lead generation, although I don't find that to be particularly robust. Let's take a look at the storage limits for awareness and comparison reasons.

The Vimeo Plus tier, their lowest paid tier, currently has a limit of 5GB of uploads per week and a total storage of 250GB for the year. That might seem like a lot (and if we were talking about text documents or even music files you might feel like that is plenty). But, consider this: One of my Entrepreneur Interview Series videos at 1080P (the minimum size/quality in my opinion) is 1.98GB. If I was to render that video at 4K (quickly becoming the new standard for video quality), its size would shoot up to 5.14GB. That 250GB of storage goes quickly if I end up uploading 4-6 times per month.

One other video hosting platform worth mentioning is Wistia. Currently, Wistia only has two tiers, a Free tier and a Pro tier. Both tiers allow you to customize their player. However, the Free tier will require the Wistia branding while the Pro tier allows you to remove their branding. Both tiers also have some basic integration with products like MailChimp, which is nice but not mission critical. If you want more advanced integration or integration with more enterprise level products, they have it, but it will cost you! The biggest difference between the Free tier and the Pro tier is the video limit.

Unlike Vimeo, Wistia does not meter your upload sizes or even your total storage. Instead, they keep it very simple with a video limit, three per month for the Free Tier and 10 per month for the Pro tier. However, you are able to upload more videos on the Pro tier only for a nominal fee. The Pro tier also carries a $100/mo. price tag which makes it the most expensive monthly option of the three platforms. Last—but certainly not least—the Wistia video analytics are pretty awesome and very insightful, so that might help justify some of that $100/month cost.

You can start to see how leveraging both YouTube and another hosting platform like Vimeo or Wistia could be a good strategy. Personally, I like the idea of having my video content on YouTube for the seachability, keyword testing, thumbnail testing, and general visibility. I also like using Vimeo or Wistia for hosting videos that might be on a landing page, or some other marketing specific tactic used to fill a lead funnel. It makes more sense to have "commercials" or "marketing videos" that might not have a broad appeal or might have a very specific purpose on your website be hosted on either Vimeo or Wistia, and have the more educational, explainer, how-to, or even the promotional type content live on YouTube. There really is no hard-set guidelines so set up some experiments and find what works best for you.

4 | FILMING PREP

It's natural to come up with an idea and immediately want to start filming. You're already busy enough, you just came up with this great idea and you don't want to lose any momentum... sound familiar?

What about this one: You start filming and what you thought would be a killer three-minute video turns into a long run-on sentence for 18 minutes because you're the "um" master, and you don't know how to wrap it up nice and tight. Frustrating!

In this chapter, I'm going to share best practices for preparing for your video shoot, including developing a video script and setting up your audio and video equipment.

SCRIPTING

There's a reason why you hear the greatest producers and directors of the films you love talk about the script. Having a solid script ahead of time allows you to practice and refine well before the camera lights come on, but it's not the most important reason for having a script. With real estate, it's location, location, location. With video content, it's story, story, story.

Let's debunk the biggest complaint I hear when it comes to scripts and stories. You CAN tell a story in three minutes or less! Say it with me again, you CAN tell a story in three minutes or less. You don't need 18 minutes, 30 minutes, or even two hours to tell a story.

I believe strongly in a story arc. With short form video content, I prefer to set story arcs using the following five key steps:

1 - Intro — This is really painting a picture of an experience the viewer should have already had, something they can easily relate to. I like to tap into the viewer's curiosity to wrap up this part and move on to Step 2.

2 - Conflict — Here we are going to further paint the picture of how something happened (or didn't happen) to them. Capitalize on the feelings here (i.e., disappointment).

3 - Light bulb moment — Here we want to paint the picture of something that sparks/sparked the beginning of a transformation—not the transformation itself, rather the "ah-ha" moment where they realized they just uncovered something or realized something powerful. (Capitalize on the feeling of hope.)

4 - Transformation — How will their perspective change or how will they physically/emotionally/mentally change? This is where we focus on the feeling of empowerment.

5 - Take Away — What is the one thing YOU want THEM to take away from this?

Using these five steps, I help my customers flesh out talking points or points of interest. From there, we discuss how we could flow easily from one section to another in a way that feels like you are telling me about something that happened to you at work yesterday. Try to make it flow smoothly. Lastly, we construct the script, but only loosely.

I'm not a big fan of crafting a lengthy, in-depth, SEO-ridden script, and for one reason: The talent never remembers it perfectly. Even if they do a good job of reciting the script, it can feel mechanical. When you can talk to the camera like your friend, the passion and authenticity comes through... and that is GOLD.

SETTING UP

Once you've created your story arc, created your talking points, and practiced, practiced, practiced it's time to set up.

I use a 4-step setup process for filming that includes a series of checks for pre-setup, setup, pre-filming, and post-filming. The pre-setup process is all about equipment and storage readiness. Prior to the day of filming, we make sure all of the camera batteries, lavalier microphone batteries, and any light batteries are fully charged. I know it seems rudimentary but—believe me when I tell you—there is no worse feeling when you go to start filming and you have 10% battery left.

Also, this process involves creating the video storage structure. I've refined my folder structure for different types of videos over the years, but they all have some of the same things in common. This is how I like to store all of the different audio, video, B-roll, pictures, and graphics to be used on the video.

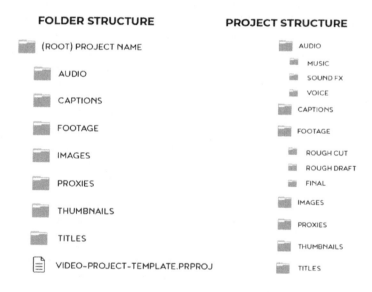

FOLDER STRUCTURE

- (ROOT) PROJECT NAME
  - AUDIO
  - CAPTIONS
  - FOOTAGE
  - IMAGES
  - PROXIES
  - THUMBNAILS
  - TITLES
  - VIDEO-PROJECT-TEMPLATE.PRPROJ

PROJECT STRUCTURE

- AUDIO
  - MUSIC
  - SOUND FX
  - VOICE
- CAPTIONS
- FOOTAGE
  - ROUGH CUT
  - ROUGH DRAFT
  - FINAL
- IMAGES
- PROXIES
- THUMBNAILS
- TITLES

During the setup process, I initially place the tripods, measure the height needed, place the lights, and dial in the zoom for what I want the video to capture. I say "initial" because nothing gets set in a final position until the subject is ready to go. Once the subject is ready, I'll maneuver the lights accordingly, change the height of the tripod, and lock in the zoom of the camera.

29

Camera Placement

Camera placement is critical and often the most overlooked and underestimated element of filming. Here are a few key points to consider with camera setup. First, make sure you are using a tripod and that tripod is level. While shaky video footage is terrible, a crooked picture that makes the viewer feel like things might just fall off the screen is pretty awful. Other things to consider with the camera tripod setup are the height and the angle.

You don't want to be too high or too low, and you certainly don't want an unflattering angle of your subject. Speaking of the subject, really think about where you want them and how you want them to place their body. Should the subject be looking directly at the camera or off camera? Would it look better if the subject is positioned at a slight angle, so they are not square with the camera? Should they be sitting or standing? All good things to think through during your setup.

Audio Setup

While what you see and the clarity of the video is very important, a clear and stable video with terrible audio is a killer. First, think through the type of microphone you want or need to use. In some cases, you have to use what you have. If you are using a lavalier mic, where should you place it so that it's inconspicuous while at the same time capturing the full range of how the subject might turn their head and speak. If you're using a boom mic, how far above the subject does it need to be in order to be out of the camera view but still close enough to capture great clarity audio? Does the subject need to move around in the video? That could sway your opinion on where to put the boom mic and whether you use a boom mic or not.

The other type of mic I typically see is an external mic mounted to the primary camera. Much like the boom mic, using these mics needs a bit of forethought around distance to the subject, background noise, etc. The one thing you don't want to do is use the onboard mic from the camera. Avoid this at all costs if you can.

Either way you go, I highly recommend you have someone listening to the audio through a dedicated set of headphones in real time. I find that as a subject or a producer, I don't always hear the echo, background noise, or low bass thumps of a toe tap as an example. But the person listening to the real-time recorded audio should be able to pick those up and let you know if you need a re-take. Not listening in real-time to the audio, only to find out there is someone walking with heavy footsteps or something is rubbing on the microphone is incredibly frustrating. It is often impossible to entirely remove in the editing process, and sometimes audio problems require a full reshoot! All things you want to and can avoid.

Lighting

Lighting is also a critical element in video, and it's something I get asked about often. There is a science to lighting, but it is also an art. Part of the science of lighting is using what is commonly referred to as *3 Point Lighting*, where there is a Key Light to illuminate the subject or primary part of the subject, a Fill Light which is a softer/dimmer light to fill in the shadowy part of the subject, and a Back Light to illuminate part of the background.

The *art* part of the lighting setup is in the placement, intensity, color, and type of lights used, among other factors. Natural light also plays a big part in lighting setup. If you're indoors and you have a window with some blinds, the natural light could cause issues when it moves throughout the day or how it is filtered, or the color could change through both the window and the blinds.

You will often see a more orange hue and texture when things like this happen. If you're outdoors during the day, the sun can wreak havoc on your filming setup. To help counteract the intensity and brightness of the sun, while also providing a more cinematic tone I like to use Neutral Density filters, or ND filters.

One quick note regarding the possible orange hue or texture you may get while shooting indoors and using filtered natural light. If this happens, it is not the end of the world! You can remove the orange tones in the video. It is not ideal, but you can do it so if this happens no need to panic.

5 | THE FILMING SESSION

I schedule and prepare all participants for our filming session(s) beforehand so they're as comfortable as possible. People tell us that our filming sessions are a lot more fun than they expected! Yours can be, too. In this chapter, I'll share some tips for a successful filming session.

I typically run through a pre-filming process. This process allows me to check audio levels of the microphone to ensure the subject's voice can be heard clearly and any other noise makers that I didn't catch with my naked ear are identified.

If the video is more of an interview style video, I will also tape up the questions (or talking points) or set up the electronic monitor where it needs to be, and make sure the "On Air" sign is lit or placed where everyone behind the camera can see it.

It is really important to also test the recording of both audio and video. Again, it seems so obvious that you wouldn't need to do this, but technology can be fickle from time to time and it's really hard to capture something magical that happened when the audio didn't record properly or the video abruptly had a focus issue, for example.

FILMING TECHNIQUES

While filming, there are a few filming techniques to be aware of and none of them require you to have gone to film school. Another way to talk about filming techniques is by using the term *cinematography*. Cinematography can be a scary word, especially when you consider people win Oscars for their brilliant work in this area. But, fear not. This does not have to be scary. In fact, this is one of my favorite parts for making the experience and the video really fun.

Cinematography is all about the visuals you use to tell the story. Aside from being somewhat skilled with operating the camera and positioning the lighting, it's about controlling what the viewer sees and experiences with how the imagery is presented to them. Following is a short list of the basics. Remember, you do not have to be an expert here, but mastering these basics will take you a long way.

Rule of Thirds

The Rule of Thirds is a concept in video and film production in which the frame is divided into three imaginary sections. The subject, or point of focus, is aligned on either side of the grid (first third or last third) rather than the center. This is not always necessary (or desirable), but it is one of those rules you should understand well before you break it.

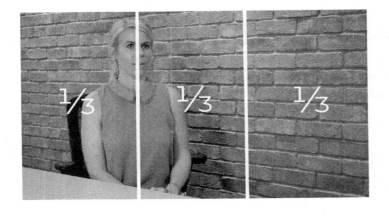

Another rule of thirds tactic is the concept of leading. This is when you place your subject on the opposite side of the frame from the object of his or her attention. This technique is psychological in nature because when your eyes look at incomplete information (such as an actor looking off-screen), they want to fill it to make it complete.

Even though there is nothing in let's say the left side of the shot, our minds automatically deduce that there is someone on the other side of that frame. If the subject had no lead room, the shot would just feel off.

180-Degree Rule

The 180-Degree Rule is a cinematography guideline that states two characters in a scene should maintain the same left/right relationship to one another. When the camera passes over the invisible axis connecting the two subjects, it is called *crossing the line*, and the shot becomes what is called a *reverse angle*.

When we watch a scene that is a two-shot of characters conversing or engaging in action like a swordfight, we notice their screen direction remains constant. If you have two subjects facing each other in the frame, imagine there is a 360-degree circle around them. Then, in your mind, cut that circle in half, creating in your mind a "line" in the center of the circle that runs between your two subjects. That is the 180-degree line which should not be crossed by the camera.

30-Degree Rule

The 30-Degree Rule is a basic film editing guideline that states the camera should move at least 30 degrees relative to the subject between successive shots of the same subject. If the camera moves less than 30 degrees, the transition between shots can look like a jump cut—which could jar the audience and take them out of the story.

Camera movement should stay on one side of the subject to follow the 180-degree rule. Otherwise, the audience might focus on the film technique rather than the narrative itself.

Headroom

Headroom refers specifically to the distance between the top of the subject's head and the top of the frame. The amount of headroom that is considered aesthetically pleasing is a dynamic quantity; it changes relative to how much of the frame is filled by the subject.

Too much room between a subject's head and the top of frame results in dead space. It's uninteresting and leaves the viewer feeling awkward.

CAMERA ANGLES

The right camera angle can have a massive impact on the story your video is telling and how your viewer is feeling. It is important to note that the shot types typically relate to the size of the subject within the shot. While there is almost an unlimited amount of possible camera angles to consider, the list below highlights some of the basic shots and the effect they have on the viewer.

- Eye Level - Shot taken with the camera approximately at eye level, resulting in a neutral effect on the audience.

- High Angle - Subject is viewed from above eye level. This can have the effect of making the subject seem vulnerable, weak, or frightened.

- Low Angle - Subject is viewed from below eye level. This can have the effect of making the subject look powerful, heroic, or dangerous.

- Tilt Angle - Shot in which the camera is set at an angle on its roll axis so that the horizon line is not level. It is often used to show a disoriented or uneasy psychological state.

- Over the Shoulder - A popular shot where a subject is shot from behind the shoulder of another, framing the subject anywhere from a Medium to Close-Up. The shoulder, neck, and/or back of the head of the subject facing away from the camera remains viewable, making the shot useful for showing reactions during conversations. It tends to place more of an emphasis on the connection between two speakers rather than the detachment or isolation that results from single shots.

- Bird's Eye View - A high-angle shot taken from directly overhead and from a distance. The shot gives the audience a wider view and is useful for showing direction and movement of the subject, to highlight spatial relations, or reveal to the audience elements outside the boundaries of the character's awareness. The shot is often taken from a crane or helicopter.

Close Up/Medium/Long Angle Shots

The list below highlights some other angle shots and the effect they have on the viewer.

- **Extreme Long Shot** - Used to show the subject from a distance, or the area in which the scene is taking place. This type of shot is particularly useful for establishing a scene (see Establishing Shot later in the article) in terms of time and place, as well as a character's physical or emotional relationship to the environment and elements within it. The character doesn't necessarily have to be viewable in this shot.

- **Long Shot** - Shows the subject from top to bottom; for a person, this would be head to toes, though not necessarily filling the frame. The character becomes more of a focus than an Extreme Long Shot, but the shot tends to still be dominated by the scenery. This shot often sets the scene and our character's place in it. This can also serve as an Establishing Shot, in lieu of an Extreme Long Shot.

- **Full Shot** - Frames the character from head to toes, with the subject roughly filling the frame. The emphasis tends to be more on action and movement rather than a character's emotional state.

- **Medium Long Shot** - Intermediate between Full Shot and Medium Shot. Shows subject from the knees up.

- **Medium Shot** - Shows part of the subject in more detail. For a person, a medium shot typically frames them from about waist up.

This is one of the most common shots seen in films, as it focuses on a character (or characters) in a scene while still showing some environment.

- **Medium Close Up** - Falls between a Medium Shot and a Close-Up, generally framing the subject from chest or shoulder up.

- **Close Up** - Fills the screen with part of the subject, such as a person's head/face. Framed this tightly, the emotions and reaction of a character dominate the scene.

- **Extreme Close Up** - Emphasizes a small area or detail of the subject, such as the eye(s) or mouth.

SETTING THE TALENT AT EASE

Now that we have a baseline of knowledge for the setup of the camera, microphone, and lighting, we need to make sure our subject is ready for filming. I call this Setting the Talent at Ease, and I have five key points I hit with every single subject I work with, that not only puts a smile on their face but also builds trust.

Anyone who hasn't been on camera before (or just isn't comfortable being on camera) wants to know what to expect. Often times, they are uneasy because they're not sure what to expect or, worse, they fear they will be judged by the person(s) behind the camera (whom they consider to be experts). The best way to combat these feelings is to set expectations early in the process. I do this as soon as the subject enters the room or filming area, and I call it an upfront contract. We talk about what is expected of them, what the equipment does and doesn't do, and where they should position themselves and look. We also talk about any queues I may give them, and I always drive home that we can, and will, take as many takes as needed.

If the video is more of an interview or testimonial type of video, then I will run them through a series of eight random questions in rapid-fire succession. I call these questions "ice breakers." I have three different types of ice breakers, but I only tell them about the last one ahead of time!

The first ice breaker is the audio test. This is where the subject is getting mic'd up, and I test their audio levels by having them tell me what they had for breakfast (and, of course, I make commentary and ask questions to keep them talking). Basically, I don't want them to be able to think too much. I just want to them to respond with the first thing that comes to mind. This tactic works wonders for nearly everyone!

Once the audio levels are dialed in, it's time to do a video check. Once again, this is both necessary in order to adjust the height of camera and placement of lights. This is also a good time for the second ice breaker where I keep the talent talking, but this time about a different subject, something they don't have to think about... usually family or a hobby. One thing this also does is help me understand how they talk, their cadence, their mannerisms and tone. This ice breaker is the only one I tell them about ahead of time.

You may be shocked to learn that sometimes people who haven't been on camera before speak differently than they would in a more casual setting!

Once we're warmed up and ready to go, it's time to film right? Wrong! It's time to run through one last practice ice breaker with lights, audio, and camera focused on the subject. Why do this? Because I find that a practice round is super helpful. First, it helps the camera operator know how the talent will move and can suggest any corrections or limitations.

Let's say, for example, that the talent was sitting still during the initial ice breakers but during the practice session, they started rocking back and forth or tapping their feet. It's important to give the talent a "free" run at the filming without having to feel the pressure of being perfect. Now, this isn't really true. Occasionally while we're recording this practice session, the talent does a phenomenal job and gives us something we want to use, allowing us to refine pieces and shorten the need for filming.

Be prepared. Some people go off script really quickly while others realize they need more, better, or different talking points.

USING MULTIPLE TAKES/CAMERAS

I like to use multiple cameras for shoots, even if it's an interview or testimonial style video. I do this for two main reasons. First, it allows me to capture different angles to break up the monotony of just seeing the talent in one specific way. Second, if something happens in the middle of a talking point or between talking points, we can pause, reset and start again and then use the footage from the second camera to make the video feel like it was a continuous take.

I also like to use multiple takes when shooting. Even if we get everything right in the first take, I prefer to shoot a second take. This gives me extra footage and material to use as part of a scene or talking points or for social media.

For videos with a lot of motion, or repeated motion, it's mandatory to use multiple takes. For example, when I record a series of CrossFit exercise movements, I instruct the talent not to "burn out" too early as we may do the same repetitive lift or movement 8-10 times—all with different camera angles or lenses. Again, this gives me more to work with during the editing process.

The last point I make with everyone involves the "script versus talking points" choice. While I want them to develop a script to capture what they want to say before we get into filming, I find that it is nearly impossible for most people to remember the script. That's the problem with scripts. You start thinking too much about what you should be saying and what part comes next.

Viewers can tell when the talent is reading a script from a teleprompter or reciting the script verbatim from memory. For this reason, I prefer to work with talking points. In an ideal situation, the talent has existing knowledge and experience, and, with the right coaching, they can talk about their experiences with much more passion if they use talking points instead of reading a script that someone else helped write. The best part about talking points is that sometimes the talent will go "off script" and talk about something that just comes natural to them around the subject matter, and that usually comes across really well.

THE IMPORTANCE OF B-ROLL

One way to really level up your videos (or to help smooth out a video with multiple cuts) is the use of B-Roll. If you think of the primary camera(s) shooting what is considered A-Roll, the secondary shots are considered B-Roll. B-Roll allows you to add a creative element to your videos to help tell the story better visually while also (secretly) hiding any video sequencing mistakes or unwanted position jumps of the talent that happened between takes.

I love using B-Roll to help with the visual narrative. Let's say you are a software company talking about your new product launch. You could use B-Roll of a stand-up Scrum meeting, or a developer coding, or even a customer using the product. Or, let's say you have a physical product and want to show customers using your product while having the time of their life in an environment that resonates with your ideal audience. The uses of B-Roll are nearly unlimited. That said, you can overuse it, so be judicious.

I prefer to shoot B-Roll in a higher frame rate than A-Roll. For example, I always shoot the primary footage for a video in 24 frames per second (FPS). I do this because this is the frame rate in which television and movies are shot, and it has the most visual appeal when viewed on traditional screens. I recommend shooting most/all the B-Roll in 60 FPS or higher.

By shooting at a higher frame rate, you'll have the ability to slow down the B-Roll footage to 24 FPS and really capitalize on the cinematic feel and smoothness of slow-motion. B-Roll is not usually shot on a tripod, which means the footage won't be as stable. This is another reason I like the higher frame rate because when I slow it down in editing, the motion blur is usually minimal.

Be sure to shoot more B-Roll than you think you need—a lot more. I can always tell when the producer of a video with B-Roll in it didn't shoot enough footage because the same or very similar clips are used more than once. Since the footage is digital, you can reuse it on future projects so it's never a waste of time.

My last tip for B-Roll is to shoot both wide-angle shots and tight-angle shots. Let's say I was shooting a street corner for B-roll. I would shoot different clips of the lamp post, the cars passing by, the lights, maybe a flashing hand sign, the curb, the buildings near the corner—all in a tight shot. Then I would go back and shoot the same things with a wide angle (and maybe from a slightly different perspective). Again, you can never have too much B-Roll, and shooting this way gives you great footage to work with for any situation.

6 | EDITING & REVISIONS

Editing is where the real magic happens. And, while I'm not a magician, I do have some advice for making sure your videos delight your audience. In this chapter, I'm going to share editing techniques that will make your videos stand out.

Before we dive in, I'd like to take a moment to remind you to have a plan in place for protecting your raw footage.

It seems obvious to save both the audio and video files to a computer, yet I can't tell you the amount of times I've heard clients who tried to do things on their own tell me they didn't immediately save the footage and lost it because they used the camera or the audio equipment for something else a day or two later and poof it vanished.

For me, it's not enough to transfer the files to a computer and be done. An important part of my process—and the part that has protected me from ever losing raw footage—involves backing up video files onto a mobile drive immediately after a recording session.

So, if you're counting, there should be three places to find the raw footage. Why? Let's say you are shooting at a remote location, such as a warehouse not far from your corporate office. You have the files on the memory card in your camera, no problem. However, when packing up your gear, something happens, and your camera gets crushed or dropped in some sort of liquid. Poof! There goes your raw footage.

Or, let's say you put your files on a laptop and someone else needs your camera for a different shoot in the next city. Hard drives never fail, right? Well, this one did, and you can't recover your footage from the laptop. Now you might be able to get the footage back from the camera, but there is no guarantee that the next camera operator won't need to format the memory card to allow enough room for the next video. The bottom line is that you can never be too safe and having one extra mobile backup just in case is worth the small amount of time it takes to transfer the files and the small amount of cost for the drive.

I can't tell you how many times someone asked me why editing takes so long or how many people have told me that they don't need editing services because they have an intern who can learn how to do it. These are both fair points, to be honest. But it's clear that these people haven't been through the editing process (or they don't have a high bar for quality). I don't say that to be elitist. I say that because I thought the same thing before I developed a passion for video production.

In some ways, I think it is a brand choice. In other ways, I think it's a misguided attempt at "quick and dirty" video production. For some companies, shaky, vertical iPhone footage might be a good fit for their brand. But for most companies, quality matters just as much as the content. And while not everyone needs (or even wants) videos that look like cinematic masterpieces, high-quality video production can play a big role in creating memorable touch points with customers.

Whether you're producing a shaky iPhone video, a cinematic feel, or somewhere in between, there are four significant elements to all video production that I feel get overlooked. I've explained each of these below.

Creating Templates and Folder Structure

It's a safe bet to consider that most of the videos you produce will be similar in nature. That is to say, most or all of them will be structured in the same way, use the same types of motion graphics, use B-Roll, and will be shot in the same setting.

One of the fastest ways to decrease editing time while making it much easier for your team of in-house editors or an external team like mine to collaborate (or even transfer editing ownership) is to create templates. The first template I prefer to start with is the folder structure template.

You will have the main camera footage, maybe a secondary camera and/or B-Roll footage, perhaps even drone or GoPro footage. Then you'll have the different audio sources, spoken audio, music and sound effects. On top of that, you could have still images and logos. And let's not forget about the motion graphics you like to use for highlighting social profiles and websites. But have you thought about where you would put third-party product files or other editing templates you my like to use? One thing I know you'll need is an easy place to store and quickly find thumbnails.

By creating a folder structure for all of your video production projects, it makes it easier to find the right files quickly and keeps everyone on the same page in terms of organization.

Templates don't just have to be folder based. When I help clients set up a new video series (or any campaign for social media), I always urge them to create templates for anything they might need to add to a video or social post. For example, I suggest creating a consistent look and feel for showing the speaker's name and title and creating a reusable graphic to display social media profile information.

Anything you have to create three or more times should be in consideration to become a template.

Editing Creativity

While this book isn't designed to go into great detail about the actual editing process, I do think some types of creative edits should be discussed.

Basic edits like J-Cuts, L-Cuts, and Match Cuts don't necessarily require pre-planning with filming prep. However, if you want to get the most out of creative edits, I strongly urge you to think about that ahead of filming and make sure you get the shots needed during filming. My two favorite creative editing cuts are: Cutting on Action and Match Cut.

- **Cutting on Action** — This is just what it sounds like. You cut at the point of action because that's what our eyes and brains are naturally expecting. When someone kicks open a door, we expect to see the change in angle when the door is kicked, not after it's flown open and swaying for a moment.

- **Match Cut** — A match cut is an edit that gives context and continuity to the scene and pushes it in a certain direction, without disorienting the viewer. You use it to either move between scenes or move around a space, while keeping everything coherent. A very basic version is shooting someone opening a door from behind, and then cutting to the opposite side as they walk through it.

I use cuts sparingly to ensure the impact of the cut is realized, but they do add a ton of value and intrigue for the viewer.

SETUP & CHECKLISTS

You're starting to see how editing effects filming, and vice versa. If you are going to do this more than once, you're going to need a process. I've provided a checklist on my site (https://fullerstory.com/checklist) to help you with planning. I used this checklist when producing each show for the Entrepreneur Series I created.

A quick backgrounder:

The Entrepreneur Series is meant to challenge the belief of what entrepreneurship looks like. The goal is to showcase other entrepreneurs, big, small, young, old, and everything in between and to shed light in areas we typically shy away from talking about. I created this series as a way to give back to all those that have helped me along the way. You can watch it at:

https://fullerstory.com/entrepreneur-series/.

Initial Video Edits

This is by far the most time-consuming set of tasks. Before I even begin editing, I start with audio cleanup and project setup. I also create video proxy files for all of my video clips. Proxy files are smaller video files that allow you to speed up the process of editing. They're basically compressed versions of the original video footage that the computer can handle far easier than the original 1080 or 4K versions. They are much smaller in file size too. When I share files with other editors on my team, we ONLY pass around the smaller video files. It's painful to pass around 8GB of video footage when I could simply create proxy files and pass around 250MB of the same footage.

The bulk of editing time will always be spent in rough cuts. This is where we comb through the raw footage and roughly stitch together the story line. Once the story line is established, the process looks like this:

Step 1: Add the B-roll.

Step 2: Mark out where any graphics might be useful.

Step 3: Identify any other creative elements needed.

When these three steps are complete, I usually move on to rough draft edits. Rough draft edits are a lot tighter than the rough cuts, but they're still not great (on purpose). This is the initial copy of the video that will be shown to the client, partner, or decision-maker for feedback. I can't tell you how many times showing a rough copy of a video to a client has saved me hours of potential headache.

Once initial feedback has been given, it's time to do the following:

- Make the precision edits

- Do color correcting

- Add graphics as needed

- Add sound effects as needed

- Dial in the audio

- Insert an intro and outro

- Render the final rough draft!

VIDEO UPLOADING...

■■■■■■■■■□□□□□□

7 | FINAL PRODUCTION

Once the client or decision-maker has seen the progress from initial rough edits to final rough edits, they should be dazzled! But don't let that go to your head. It's about the storyline and making sure it is on point.

I typically allow one last round of edits (the second round) before finalizing the video. Depending on the needs, purpose, and usage of the video, the finalization process could require the addition of captions and multiple video file outputs for different platforms and needs.

In either scenario, it's wise to create a video thumbnail (i.e., still image from the video) to be used with the video upload or placed in the video as the first frame. This ensures that the video thumbnail will be something the client/decision-maker wants to have viewers see when they navigate to the place in which the video lives (such as on a website).

PRO TIP: You don't want to be at the mercy of being forced to use either the first frame of the video or a frame chosen for you by whichever hosting platform you're using. Many times, the first frame doesn't convey what the video is about and if it's a talking head or interview video it probably shows someone just about to say "Hi" with a scrunched-up face. Not the way you get visitors to really want to watch your video!

CREATING SOCIAL MEDIA ASSETS

This part of a video project is often overlooked or becomes an afterthought once the video has been posted for all to see. This process can be a bit daunting at first as it requires both input from the client/decision-maker as well as different editing to accommodate the platform of choice.

Preparing a video for use on social media requires additional video outputs rendered specifically for each of the different social platforms (Facebook, Twitter, LinkedIn, etc.). It's not uncommon for me to have rendered over 10 different assets at the conclusion of a project based on the type of video and platforms on which they'll be shared. Keep in mind that you will likely need to create still frames of the video (i.e., thumbnails) for image posts as well.

See the latest formatting requirements for sharing videos on social platforms at http://www.fullerstory.com/social.

VIDEO UPLOAD & LAUNCH PREP

Now that we have the video completed and everyone is happy, it's time to upload and go... right? Not so fast! Depending on where you upload your video, there are key steps to include in the upload and launch readiness process.

I leverage the power of YouTube, but I also want to control the user experience. That's to say the video lives on YouTube so I can benefit from the built-in search and SEO capabilities. However, I also want those browsing my website to see the videos without having to leave the website.

YouTube provides the ability to embed the video on a webpage simply by using their native embed code. This code is specific to the video and even allows YouTube analytics to track views, watch time, and differentiate whether it was watched natively in YouTube or via an external source (i.e., my website). But in order to leverage the search power of YouTube, you need to do more than just upload your video. The thumbnail and title you use for your video are critical factors in your video's "findability" on the YouTube platform (as well as in Google search results). The video description and associated tags are also very important and help with SEO, but having a compelling thumbnail and a catchy title prove time and time again to be GOLD.

In addition to uploading to YouTube, I personally love to create a dedicated page for the video with plenty of copy that will help generate value from an SEO perspective. Depending on the type of video, I may add a transcription of the video (or a modified transcription tailored like a blog post) as well as a timeline and topics discussed for interview style videos—or even links to equipment and/or products used in the video.

THUMBNAILS

The inexact science part of the editing process is the creation of thumbnails. The word alone, thumbnail, just seems so simple and small and easy to do, yet so important!

Heed my warning: Do not underestimate the thumbnail! The two biggest mistakes I see most businesses employ when it comes to thumbnails are: 1) not creating a separate thumbnail specifically for use in either social media or their webpage, and 2) not understanding what their audience gravitates toward when it comes to grabbing their attention.

Most places where you will want to show your video will select the thumbnail for you when you upload the video file or add a reference URL. You've seen it before. You go to a website, it has a video right there on the home page (something they worked really hard on and put a lot of love and effort into), and the image for the video, or thumbnail, is a person with their mouth half open or with a drunken gaze on their face. Gasp!

What is going on here?! Not only is that a terrible first impression, but it's embarrassing to the talent—and let's hope it isn't a customer testimonial!

It's a little-known fact, but most platforms do not know what image within your video will make someone want to watch it. They simply display the very first frame of the video as the thumbnail. Some video editors either fade into a video (making the thumbnail black) or cut the beginning so tight that the viewer is dropped right into the message. In either scenario, your new thumbnail is not what you want and most certainly doesn't represent the pure genius of your video.

YouTube and Facebook have a feature that allows you to select from a series of frames that they provide you as a thumbnail. It's a start, but it's still not ideal. Instead, I prefer to craft a custom thumbnail that can be added to the very beginning of the video as a single frame image. This gives me the ability to create a single image that is visually appealing and helps inform the viewer what they are about to watch. A good thumbnail is imperative for grabbing a viewer's attention.

Grabbing the attention of viewers requires more than just a thumbnail image, of course. Thumbnails are the non-verbal, non-written communication part of the equation for grabbing attention, and it's usually the first thing viewers see and comprehend quickly. Crafting a clever title for the video is also critical. Think about it. You see a picture of a cute puppy jumping through a flaming hoop suspended in the air. Ok. That's interesting. But then you look at the title, and it reads "How to train your dog to follow commands in 5 easy steps." You got me!

For starters, I want to know how to train my dog. And to think I could train my dog to jump through a hoop—let alone a hoop on fire! —in five easy steps… yeah, I'll click on that. Now let's imagine the title read, "How to teach your dog to breathe fire." You're not clicking on that.

The last step in the thumbnail trifecta is the description. The description is exactly what it sounds like. It's a place where you can go into a bit more detail about the video. You can use this for calling out reference points, or highlighting external links that may be talked about in the video. You can even use it to identify a quick timeline so the viewer can have more insight into what is talked about and when. However, you use it, consider that the description's real value is for search engine optimization (SEO).

8 | VIDEO MARKETING

There are almost five billion videos watched on YouTube every day. My goal isn't to teach you how to make your video "go viral." My goal is to help you get your video content in front of the right people at the right time. That always involves spending time and often involves spending money.

The same best practices marketers (like us) have used to help our message rise above the noise applies to video as well: Produce compelling content and give people a reason (and a way) to engage with you through it.

In this chapter, I'll share some best practices for increasing the visibility of your videos and using videos in advertising campaigns.

OPTIMIZING VIDEOS FOR SEARCH ENGINE VISIBILITY

If you're an online marketer, you probably have at least a basic understanding of how content such as articles and blog posts are used to attract visitors to a website. In much the same way, video content can be used to attract search engine users—and it can often be more effective.

You'll find that videos often display at the top of search engine results before organic, text-based results. The tactics used to rank high on results pages are similar to those used for landing page ranking, but there are some additional ones to consider.

First, where you host your videos will impact your visibility on search engines. I recommend publishing your videos on both YouTube and Vimeo. I've found that YouTube videos earn better placement on search engine results pages, but Vimeo videos look better (and your visitor will never see anyone else's ads.) Both YouTube and Vimeo make publishing your videos on social networking sites like Facebook, Twitter, and LinkedIn easy. Both platforms provide performance dashboards so you can track video engagement. For $50/month, Vimeo lets you add a call-to-action and collect email addresses within the video player.

Make sure to create a YouTube channel with playlists so you can control the user experience as much as possible. And, unless it's part of your revenue stream, turn off ads for your channel as well.

Next, make sure that you add captions to your videos. Video captions are a good practice for ensuring accessibility for people with disabilities, and they also act as crawlable text for search engines. In addition, having the option to mute a video means your viewers can avoid annoying their office mates (or, ahem, multitask during conference calls).

Similar to optimizing other types of content (such as blog posts), the title and description you use for your video should contain keyword(s) that your target audience is using in their search. But avoid keyword stuffing (i.e., filling your title and/or description with several keywords). Remember that a human must be compelled to click on the link to you watch your video. If you're embedding the video on a landing page, make sure that the landing page is optimized using the same keywords. Keep in mind that Google usually only indexes one video per page, so embed your most important video near the top of the page.

As I mentioned previously, make sure to use an attention-grabbing thumbnail. The thumbnail is shown in the search results and can make a big impact on your search engine click-through rates. Studies show that thumbnails featuring an image of a person get a 30% higher video play rate. Some argue that it's more important than the title!

PROMOTING VIDEOS IN ADVERTISING CAMPAIGNS

Video advertising as a marketing tactic can work very well for any type of organization, regardless of company size or product/service they're promoting. Per eMarketer, US mobile ad spending will outstrip all traditional media ad spending combined by 2020. It is estimated that US mobile video ad spending will total $15.93 billion in 2019, with that figure swelling to $24.81 billion by 2022. This growth is driven by mobile video content viewership.

You can create video-based advertising campaigns on a number of advertising platforms, from Google and YouTube to social sites like Facebook, LinkedIn, and Twitter too. In fact, marketers use the same advertiser interface to run video-based ads as they do standard paid search/display and social ads. The only difference is that you use the video as the creative.

Since Google owns YouTube, you'll use AdWords to run video ads within the Google network and on YouTube. For social sites like Facebook or Twitter, you simply upload the video you want to use in the ad and choose your targeting and budget requirements as you would with any paid social advertising campaigns.

It's important to consider that viewing video ads within native environments (where ads appear like the regular content) improves video performance metrics. That's why advertising using video is so effective on sites like Facebook and LinkedIn.

Types of Video Ads

There are a number of ways to use video content in advertising. You can download a tip sheet containing the latest trends on my site at https://fullerstory.com/videoads, but I cover a few of the most common types below.

In-Stream Video Ads

In-stream video ads are the most common type of video ad. These are short ads that play before (pre-roll), during (mid-roll), or after (post-roll) someone else's piece of video content. Linear ads are 15-30 seconds long. The viewer cannot fast forward through them. You use either 16:9 or 4:3 aspect ratio for these ads (16:9 is the most common). Non-linear ads run simultaneously with video content and will sometimes overlay the main video content.

Outstream Video Ads

A newer form of video advertising is the "outstream video" (also called native video). An outstream video is a video ad unit that automatically plays when a user scrolls near it within text-based content (such as an article). It's called outstream because the video ad exists outside of online video content (i.e., it's not a pre-roll or mid-roll ad that plays within an existing video).

This ad format is unique in that it does not require a publisher's video for placement, making it a far more flexible ad format to use. These types of video ads are capable of achieving 100% viewability and are watched 25% longer than other types of video ads.

Also, outstream ads only play when a user action takes place on the page. These actions cannot be faked by bots, so you don't have to worry about ad fraud.

Interactive Video Ads

Interactive video ads are designed to encourage viewer engagement. These video ads take over the entire screen of whatever device your viewer is using. You can provide different ways for users to engage with these types of ads, such as enable them to sign up for notifications or click to order something.

In-Game Video Ads

In-Game video ads display while a computer or video game is loading, or the player is in-between levels in the game. This is a common way for mobile game makers to monetize their users without having to charge them to play/install their game. These types of ads are effective for game makers, but other types of organizations should keep close tabs on "accidental clicks," which can happen often.

Google/YouTube In-Stream Advertising

In-stream video ads are "skippable" and can appear on YouTube watch pages, on videos on partner sites, and mobile apps in the Google Display Network. These videos should be 12-30 seconds long. Keep in mind that your video must be hosted on YouTube to use it for advertising campaigns on Google.

When running video ad campaigns in Google, you can bid two different ways: 1) **CPV** (cost per view), or 2) **CPM** (cost per 1,000 views), With CPV, you pay when a viewer watches at least 30 seconds of your video (or the whole video if it's shorter than 30 seconds). With CPM, you pay based on impressions. More specifically, you pay each time your ad is shown 1,000 times.

Micro Video Ads

While 30-second videos are still common, the current trend is to use 10-second micro video ads to capture the viewer's attention as part of a multi-touch marketing program. You can use micro-videos on the platform of your choice.

Video in Remarketing Campaigns

Remarketing campaigns are used to show ads to people who have already visited your website (or your app). You can use videos in your remarketing campaigns just as you would in a typical Display Network or Search Network campaign.

Video remarketing enables you to market videos to people based on their specific behaviors, such as their video viewing history, their engagement on your website or social channels, and even their video channel subscriptions. These details filter a potential audience, so you can display your videos to the most relevant consumers.

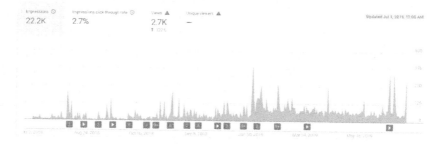

9 | MEASURING SUCCESS

The third most popular question I am asked from business leaders is, "How can we measure the performance of our videos?"

Most marketing companies and marketing teams will push for the use of "marketing metrics." Many of them will prefer to measure video performance in leads and conversions. While I don't disagree that the ultimate goal for viewers who are not already customers is to convert them into customers, it's never as linear as that.

Instead of thinking about video performance in terms of leads and conversions, consider thinking about your video content performance in terms of engagement with and the value to your customer. That is ultimately why you're creating videos in the first place, right?

Most people who are searching for what you do know they have a problem and they're looking for a solution. Or maybe they don't have a problem yet and they are just looking for information from a credible source. Your job is to create videos that help them acquire the information they seek in a very consumable way and to provide them with knowledge and/or education around how they could solve the problem.

You want to create AWARENESS that you are the credible source and build TRUST by providing them information they seek so you can be seen as an AUTHORITY in this area of expertise. That way, when they are ready to make a purchase, they COMMIT to the product or service you're offering. And, when everything goes right, they instinctually recommend you to everyone they know. So how do you measure that?

Here are a few measurements to consider:

- **Impressions** — This is the number of times a video was available for viewing. Impression counts each time a person sees your content, so one viewer can generate multiple impressions.

- **Number of Views** — This is the number of times the video is viewed. Depending on the hosting platform, a view could be counted if at least three seconds of the video is watched. This can also be described as the "play rate." Play rate is based on how many people play your video divided by the number of people who visit the page that hosts your video.

- **Watch Time or Retention Time** — This is the length of time the viewer spends watching your video. This is usually communicated in both minutes/seconds and percentage. Ideally, you want to keep your audience for a minimum of 45% of the total duration of the video. This metric measures your video's ability to hold a viewer's attention.

- **Number of Videos Viewed** — This is the number of videos the viewer watched in either a single session or during multiple sessions. This metric could be a great indicator as to how valuable your overall content is for your ideal customer.

- **Click-Through Rate** — This metric is presented as a percentage and measures how well your video encourages viewers to take a desired action. This desired action is called a "call-to-action." **Tip:** Test using a call-to-action in different places in your video.

- **Engagement Rate** — This metric is presented as a percentage and measures how much your audience engages with your video content. Engagement is usually based on the number of comments, likes, and reactions a video post receives. Tip: Engagement rate is one of the most important factors in boosting your video's organic reach on social platforms like Facebook.

VIDEO ADVERTISING METRICS

When it comes to measuring the return on paid advertising campaigns, it's important to consider additional metrics. And, yes, conversion rate must be one of them. I describe additional metrics to track below.

- **Cost Per View** — This number represents the fee you paid for one view of your video. A view is counted when a viewer watches 30 seconds of your video ad (or the duration if it's shorter than 30 seconds) or interacts with the ad, whichever comes first.

- **Reach** — This number shows the total number of people who saw your video over a given time period. Unlike impressions where one person can generate multiple impressions, each unique viewer is only counted one time.

- **Frequency** — This is the average number of times a unique person is shown your ad over a given time period. Tip: Try to keep this number under seven (7) views.

- **Conversion Rate** — Your video's conversion rate is presented as a percentage. It measures how well your video persuaded viewers to complete a desired call-to-action within the video (such as clicking a button to request more information on your website).

10 | TIPS, TRICKS & BEST PRACTICES

It doesn't matter what I'm doing, if I can find someone experienced enough to share their thoughts, any best practices, or tricks they've learned—I'm all ears! So, I've decided to do the same here. Below are some items that I feel are great to know about, even if you don't immediately put them into practice.

MANAGING FEEDBACK WHILE EDITING

Most of the time, my clients are eager to push out video content as soon as they can get their hands on the finished product. One way we help them get there and ensure they love the end product is coach them through the editing and revision process.

There isn't necessarily a wrong way for a client to share feedback and edit requests. However, there are ways to ensure the feedback is received correctly in order to minimize the time it takes to make the revisions and get the final version.

Let's say a client didn't like the intro to a video. They might reply with, "I'm not a fan of the intro." To some people, that might mean cut it all together; to others, it's an unfinished statement and requires more discussion.

What would happen if they actually said, "I'd cut out all front office intros and cut from Bonnie at about thirty seconds after she says, 'students succeed'?"

Talk about specific! This is great feedback! It is very specific, has time stamps, and contains a reference to what is being said. What is being said coupled with the time stamp is incredibly helpful. Some videos are very wordy and not everyone takes a razor-sharp view of the time at which the word or phrase is spoken. Sometimes thirty seconds is really twenty seconds, which doesn't seem like a big deal until there is a critical spoken component from :27 to :30!

Here is another example that comes up over and over: The on-screen talent (Debbie in this case) struggles to remember what she is trying to say next and naturally says "and um" a few more times than she would like. Thankfully, in this case, we captured a lot of B-roll. A great way to provide feedback in this case would be to say something like this: "I would start with Debbie's intro to the tech lab, use more B-roll to cover up the 'ums', then cut at 1:04 when she says '...we are so excited...' and pick up at 1:19 when she says '... daily basis'." Again, this is very specific feedback, and the client has demonstrated that they're aware that we had B-roll to use in strategic ways like this.

TWO REVISIONS OR LESS

Another question I get quite often from both prospective clients and existing clients is about revisions. *How many revisions do we get?*

You should not need more than two rounds of video editing revisions. If you are the producing company, assuming you prepared well, the client shouldn't be surprised by the initial rough draft.

By the time you get to the revisions stage in the production process, both the video producer and the client/customer would have already defined the video content strategy and discussed the type of visuals you are all expecting to see. Ideally, that all happened before you even started shooting the video. Once the filming process has started, the video producer should have coached you through the filming process—both with your presence on camera and with the content. All of this should make the editing process very streamlined.

As the client/customer, you should share your feedback on the rough draft content then again after the final production has been put together.

During final production, you'll want to address the minutia. If you need more revisions after this, there is a very good chance something was missed, miscommunicated, or just flat out wrong prior to the editing process.

THE PAYMENT CYCLE

All up front, all at delivery, half and half. Let me explain why there's only one method that works well for you, the customer.

I have found over the years that you never want to mess with your employees' pay or their parking! Even a legitimate mistake can become very emotional. Don't believe me? Try taking away an employee's normal parking space and see what happens! When it comes to clients, it works much the same way.

As a producer, it would be great to get all the money up front. But that's unrealistic because your client might feel like they don't have any leverage if you disappear, do a bad job, or just flake out. A client might want to wait to write a check when the final video is produced, but that's too risky for you, the producer. There's is a lot of work that has to be done before filming, during editing, and in final production. And, let's be honest, if you don't have skin in the game, the waiting game of feedback can be weeks instead of days. What should take 2-4 weeks now takes 6-8 weeks. It seems far-fetched, but it happens all of the time.

I find that to create more of a "we're in this together" feel, billing 50% upfront before shooting starts and the other 50% to be due at time the finished video is released is a great way to keep everything clean and simple.

COMMON ISSUES WHILE FILMING

Here are a few common issues that happen from time to time while filming and what you can do about them.

Bad Lighting

Bad lighting—this is the worst! There is no such thing as enough lighting. Keep in mind you don't have to use all of the lighting but having it could mean the difference between a decent video and a great video.

Bad lighting can result in a fuzzy picture, deep shadows, or just a video that is too dark to watch. One way to reduce the likelihood of bad lighting is to do a test shoot ahead of time.

For example, when I scout locations, I may also schedule a little time to do a test shoot during or around the same time of day that we would be doing the real video shoot. This way we can setup the lighting and camera, play with angles, amount of lights, placement of lights, and most importantly recording something and getting it into editing to see how it looks and what we may want to change prior to the real shoot. This, of course, takes time and isn't always feasible which is why we also schedule time ahead of the real shoot for a lighter version of testing. Nine times out of 10, we make slight adjustments that really make a difference.

Natural Color Is Orange

This happens quite a bit when shooting in front of a window or when a window in the room isn't covered or filtered. The best way to avoid this is to cover the window, but that isn't always feasible. Also, you may not see an issue when you first start shooting but as the location of the sun changes the color might creep in. This will most likely be something your eye doesn't catch. If this happens, do not fear and definitely do not throw away your video footage.

There are ways to remove or diminish the orange color in editing. It may not be perfect, but it will absolutely work. I can't tell you the amount of times I get a panicked call about how the location was perfect, the scenery was amazing, but the video came out with this awful orange filter on it. By the time we're done editing, the very same person can't believe their eyes! Best not to have to rely on post-production editing, but it is there when you need it.

Camera Focus Issues

The best thing about modern day cameras is autofocus, and the worst thing about modern day cameras can be autofocus. Autofocusing problems fall into the "It doesn't happen often, but when it does it makes you want to scream" category.

Sometimes this happens when you're filming with two subjects and one of the subjects moves enough where the autofocus wants to constantly change, resulting in a fuzzy picture. You could always turn auto-focus off, but that presents its own challenges in setup, and knowing more about the camera than you'd probably like to.

I find that the best way to mitigate this issue is to both have a test shoot (even for five minutes) to make sure all of the equipment is playing nicely, and also to have someone behind the camera keeping an eye on the subjects and the focus.

Audio Problems

When you use wireless lavalieres, there is always a chance of a split-second "glitch" or audio cut out. It doesn't happen very often, but it does happen. In fact, I've even had it happen with wired lavalieres, although the issue was more related to the battery than the wires. Either way, if you don't have someone with headphones on monitoring the audio you won't catch it until it's time for editing.

Another common audio problem is forgetting to record the audio. (This is my personal favorite because it happens to us all—but usually only once!) Depending on your audio setup, you may record directly into an external device or perhaps directly into a computer. In either setup, both the device and computer have a special "record" feature.

It sounds obvious, but the tricky part about this is that you can hear the audio from the subject, but it won't start recording until you actually hit the record button. Many times, you'll be moving fast. You'll be checking audio levels (not recording), move on to something else and then *Action!* Before you know it, your subject is saying the most profound thing you've ever heard, and you didn't record any of it. Again, if you have someone monitoring the camera focus, and the audio, you can also have them double-check that the recording light is on! Don't laugh too hard. I can't tell you how many times someone has told me that this happened to them.

It is amazing the amount and range of sounds we don't hear (or are unaware of). One of biggest complaints I hear is about background noise. Our ears and our senses don't hear the air conditioning unit anymore—or the low thumping of someone tapping their feet. You know what does pick those up as loud as ever? The microphone!

Much like post-production can be used for video clean up, it can also be used for audio clean up. However, there are always prices to pay for cleaning up things like background noise. It's best to try and eliminate or avoid where possible... or even to plan for and include the ambient noise into your video if it makes sense.

One way I like to check the sounds is during the location scouting and/or setup process. I've been known to bring an external recorder with me and just leave it out while I walk around or while I'm checking out a space. After I'm done, I'll just let it play back and better yet, I toss the audio into an editor and see what kind of background noise I'm dealing with. Knowing before you shoot is always better than not knowing!

Breaking the Fourth Wall

It can be really hard not to look at the camera when filming. Let's be honest, there is a big stack of equipment pointed right at you and you're so used to "smiling for the camera" that you just have to sneak a peek.

When this happens, it's called breaking the 4th wall. In some video content you want to speak directly to the viewer, but in others you want to pretend the viewer is "listening in on the conversation." In that case you never want your subject to look directly at the camera.

One way I work with subjects to avoid this mistake is to sit directly in front of them and have them talk to me as if we were just having a conversation. I get them to focus on me and not the camera. The side benefit to this is that they typically relax and let their personality shine through when they feel like it's just the two of us. And YES, I will often tell a little white lie that the camera isn't even on, that we're just running through it one time before we do it "for real"! Sneaky, I know.

Another way I help the subject avoid this mistake is to setup a second camera. Not for them to look at, but when they do look at camera 1, we can cut to camera 2 in the editing process and it looks seamless.

FILMING SEQUENCE

Filming sequences do not have to be in order. This throws everyone for a loop the first time. The video will be seen in the right order, but that doesn't mean you have to shoot it in the same order.

Breaking up the shooting can be very helpful for time constraints. If we're filming and the CEO has a part to play, then we can shoot that part of the video whenever they have time and shoot the rest of the video around that. Or better yet, if you are shooting a series of videos you could batch them, then edit them together as needed later.

COMMON ISSUES WHILE EDITING

The editing process takes too long. This isn't really an issue, it's more of a reality. It would be nice to film for 3 hours, and only need another 3 hours to produce a great video... but that's just not how it typically works out! The editing process is just that, a process.

One way to combat editing fatigue is to break up the process into three parts. The first part of the editing process is called the rough cut. This is where we take the raw footage and put it together in a way that tells the story, outlined in the very beginning of the process.

You have to cut down all of the footage, audio, B-roll, imagery into something that "could" be used. It doesn't mean it will make the final cut, but it needs to be put into a sequence to ensure you have what you need, and it is relatively coherent.

One thing to note here, is that there are NO EDITS DONE here, other than remove unneeded footage. Most of the time, the client or decision maker doesn't see the outcome of this process, mainly because it is so raw it would leave them wondering what they just paid for.

Once the rough cut is done, we move on to the rough draft. The rough draft has tighter edits for both the audio and the footage, while also incorporating some color enhancement, among other things. The client or decision maker does get to see this output, and feedback is absolutely required at this stage.

Once the feedback has been given, reviewed, and accepted, the final production happens. This process may tweak all elements of the video, from color to background music, add vocals to any motion graphics that will be displayed. Since we are adding and editing, I typically like to ask for feedback one more time just to ensure nothing was missed.

THE IMPORTANCE OF HAVING A PROCESS

Another reason why video production might "take too long" is because you don't have a solidified process. Throughout this book you should have been able to pick up on the fact that there should be a process for each step in the production and that each step has a significant dependency on at least one previous step.

Your process doesn't have to be perfect. In fact, it's better that it's not initially because you want to find what works for you and your situation. But, once you have a process dialed in, it is amazing how quickly you can go from idea to filming to final product.

B-ROLL

You can NEVER have enough B-roll material. Period. I can't stress this enough. This is a case where you should purposely have more than you think you could possibly use, because you never know how you will end up using it or where you might also need it.

For reference, I could shoot B-roll of a street corner for an hour between different angles, different vantage points, having a narrow focus, having a wide focus, shooting up toward the sky, shooting down from high above, shooting with a rotation motion, shooting with a pan motion... you get the point!

OVERUSE/UNDERUSE OF CREATIVE EDITS

There are a few times when the video should be more about the creative edits and less about the story, but very few. Creative edits and motion graphics should add value to the video, not overtake it or take away from the purpose (the story).

Personally, I see this a lot with new video departments or inexperienced video companies. They don't do a great job with the story or the filming and "make up for it" with over-the-top editing and graphics that fly around and pop in and out of the screen. Don't fall into this trap.

REUSING CONTENT

Anything that you film, shoot, or record should always have an intended reuse. Before you even setup a camera or plug in a microphone you should have already been thinking and planning how you could "also" use this content. Whether it be for a separate podcast, social media video, social media post, or even an audiogram, I have yet to produce content that couldn't have a dual use... it's just efficient!

CONTENT INTRO

The experts say you have about 10 seconds to really capture someone's attention before they will commit to watching your video, and they're right. How does this affect you? Well, it means that not only do your videos need to provide some sort of value, but they also need a really good intro to hook the viewer.

Now, there are a lot of different ways to create an intro and you'll have to experiment with what works for you as well as what works for your audience. For example, if your videos are educational in nature and in the legal field and you are a cross between funny and laid back, then opening your videos with an in-your-face, high-intensity drill sergeant type of intro probably won't work for you. Plus, it's not authentic, and people will see through it really fast. On the other hand, you can't afford to be monotonously boring or just jump right into the content and not let the viewer know what the video content is all about and set their expectations.

DON'T MAKE A VIDEO; PRODUCE A STORY

Throughout this entire book, I've talked about video production. But the truth is that if you focus on just creating videos, you're going to fail. It's not just about the content of your videos; it's about the story you can and will tell. So instead of producing videos, produce stories! It's why I didn't name my company Fuller Video Production.

11 | GEAR, SOFTWARE &
OTHER RESOURCES

In this chapter, I will list some of the software and other resources that I recommend using for video production. I also maintain an updated list of my favorite gear on my kit page at https://kit.com/fullerstory.

Gear, Setup, and Options

Rev.com

This online tool is amazing for creating captions and transcriptions. For $1/minute how could you go wrong! Whether you use it for captions on the videos and/or social media video posts, or you use it for transcribing your video to also publish a blog post, this tool is GOLD.

Video Hive

Part of the Envato Marketplace, Video Hive is like a candy store. They have an incredible selection of templates, graphics, or motion graphics to choose from. Whether you need something quick that still looks professional, or you like to have ready-made options, this marketplace will deliver.

Motion Array

A lot like Video Hive, you can grab templates and stock artifacts. Personally, I like Video Hive better for most things, but Motion Array is a SOLID backup.

TubeBuddy

If you're going to host your video content on YouTube, you'll want to explore either TubeBuddy or VidID. Tubebuddy not only gives you analytics and insights into how well your video or videos are doing, but it also has a pretty good content brainstorm solution that just might be the difference maker with SEO on your videos.

VidID

Much like TubeBuddy, VidID has a lot of the same features and is a solid backup if you ever need it. Right now, I really like the VidIQ keyword tool.

CustomThumbnails.com

Full disclosure, I met the owner of Customthumbnails.com at a conference and didn't even know that something like this existed. Their ability to help you create a great thumbnail is nearly second to none. Fast turnaround times, and at a price that nearly makes you wonder how you couldn't go this route.

LibSyn

There are a lot of podcast hosting and syndication apps out there. The easiest one to use is LibSyn. From the setup to the upload and publish process, this tool is easy to understand and use. It's not the flashiest product, but man does it work well.

Trello

A free tool to help me stay organized, yes please! I personally love Trello for its ability to act like a Scrum board so I can quickly see progress, setup template cards and checklists.

Evernote

Evernote is probably the tool I use the absolute most. It's free, great for capturing ideas, scripts, and shot lists. It has a mobile component and the ability to share notes. The latest feature is its ability to create reusable templates... talk about a tool that actually saves you time and brain power!

Adobe Spark

Not as widely known as Canva, but very powerful. Whether I'm creating thumbnails for videos, social posts, or even just grabbing some stellar stock photography, Adobe Spark is an essential go-to for me.

Canva

Probably the most commonly used tool for graphics, social posts, and thumbnails, Canva is a solid option. I moved away from Canva personally when I was testing Adobe Spark and haven't looked back. If you don't have Adobe Spark, Canva is a must have.

Software

Adobe Creative Suite

I use five different Adobe Creative Suite products daily. 1) Premiere Pro for video editing, 2) Audition for audio recording and clean up, 3) After Effects for 3D objects and motion graphics among other things, 4) LightRoom for photo editing, and 5) Photoshop for photo manipulation and thumbnail production.

Camtasia

Pretty good tool for screen capture, and maybe some light editing depending on your need and skill level.

ScreenFlow

I recently moved from Camtasia to ScreenFlow as I'm testing other options for great screen recording. So far, this product has not disappointed.

Music and Stock Images/Video

Epidemic Sound

My absolute favorite place to get music for videos. The wide range of options with vocals or without in every mood and genre is amazing.

MusicBed

To be honest, I have not tried MusicBed—mainly because I am so happy with Epidemic Sound. However, some of the people I collaborate with love it, and I wanted to give you another option.

SoundSnap

BEST PLACE TO GET SOUND EFFECTS, period.

ABOUT THE AUTHOR

My name is Patrick, and this is my Fuller Story.

This year (2019) I celebrated my 13th wedding anniversary to the love of my life, Joy. We have two children, Preston (9) and Cassidy (6) and no pets… although let's be honest, that'll change! I have a younger sister, Kristin, who is a fantastic aunt and both of my parents are recently retired.

I was an athlete through high school, and only discovered computers in college after I had a serious wrist injury. I fell in love at first key stroke and was just amazed at how computers and the internet could be used. My very first "big boy" job was in a small technical consulting company focused on custom software development. They slid a 400+ page book about the .NET framework and C# language across my desk and said, "read up, you start at a client on Monday"… I kid you not! I spent the next 10 years honing my programming skills, analysis skills, and project management skills and loved every minute of it.

My passion and excitement for technology eventually shifted to business and after a few pain staking years of feeling alone and isolated to do the entrepreneur thing on my own I found a group of other entrepreneurs that changed my life. The group is called Entrepreneurs Organization and is a worldwide organization with localized chapters all over. In 2010, I started a professional services company focused on providing project management and application development expertise. As the CEO, I knew that focusing on optimizing profitability was important for the longevity of the business, so I developed a software application to make forecasting and scoping our projects much easier. With this new software in place, our profitability skyrocketed (and we didn't have to increase our rates).

What started out as a home-grown tool quickly evolved into a new product—and a new company! —called ForeIQ. We knew we had a great solution for other professional services firms like ours, but we weren't sure how to market it effectively. How do we explain the benefits of using business forecasting to people in a Facebook ad? How do we demonstrate how powerful—yet simple—this software is? These were the questions that plagued me. Then the answer became obvious: We needed to make a video that explained why we created this product. In other words, I needed to share my story. However, there was a small problem: Video strategy and production were foreign to me. But I decided to dive in deep and learn about both. First, I created a video that explained my backstory. Then I produced a series of project management videos and product training videos to help people understand what it is that we built and how they could use it to improve profitability on their projects. People loved them. The best thing about this video project was that I had a total blast! I caught the bug for telling stories through video, and I made a decision to help others do the same.

I didn't know it at the time, but this evolution started to change my life in other ways as well. I started to get "off the couch" so to speak and get back into being an athlete. I joined a CrossFit gym (CrossFit box for the purists), found an amazing coach and continue to work at it every single day.

Now, helping business leaders and entrepreneurs tell their story has become a passion for me. In fact, I developed the Fuller Entrepreneur Series in which I interview other entrepreneurs in an attempt to challenge the belief about what entrepreneurship looks like. I've worked with a lot of people to help them share their unique stories and create great content.

I'm not sure what the next chapter will bring (get it, next chapter!) but I know I love doing what I'm doing, and I hope to continue creating great content and helping others.

Learn more about Fuller Story at https://fullerstory.com.